M.C. LAYTON.

D0718129

THE VAN EYCKS
HUBERT AND JAN

The World's Masters ~ New Series

by Anthony Bertram

THE STUDIO PUBLICATIONS, LONDON & NEW YORK

FIRST PUBLISHED 1950

WORLD'S MASTERS NEW SERIES *Editor: ANTHONY BERTRAM*

The covers of this series, designed by Arthur Hundleby, are based on heraldic motives representing the national school to which each artist belongs or with which he is chiefly associated

Already published

WILLIAM BLAKE

SANDRO BOTTICELLI

JAN VERMEER OF DELFT

HANS HOLBEIN THE YOUNGER

WILLIAM HOGARTH

JEAN AUGUSTE DOMINIQUE INGRES

PIERO DELLA FRANCESCA

EL GRECO

MICHELANGELO

PIETER BRUEGEL

MATHIAS GRÜNEWALD

EUGENE DELACROIX

HIERONYMUS BOSCH

Others in preparation

Printed in Great Britain by William Clowes & Sons Ltd, London and Beccles. Published in London by The Studio Ltd, 66 Chandos Place, WC2, and in New York by the Studio Publications Inc, 381 Fourth Avenue

Introduction

THE beauty of the works called 'van Eycks', and their high importance in the history of Northern painting, are never questioned; but there is very little information about their authorship or their technique that is not. The student soon discovers that the familiar legend, what 'everybody knows' about the van Eycks, is the most insubstantial of pageants; and when it has faded, only a few rather insignificant facts and a great many disputed theories are left behind. I have neither the competence nor the wish to get involved in these theories, but I must at least say something of the two main problems.

The first concerns authorship. There is, in the church of St Bavon at Ghent, a most celebrated altarpiece—*The Holy Lamb*. On the frame of the lower panels the following inscription is painted:

> P(ictor) Hubertus (e) Eyck maior quo nemo repertus
> Incepit pondusz(que) Johannes arte secundus
> P(er)fecit. Judoci Vijd prece fretus
> VersV seXta MaI Vos CoLLoCat aCta tVerI.

The bracketed letters are missing. The capital letters of the last line make a chronogram of the date 1432. (Rearranged, they give: MCCCLLXVVVVII). The inscription may therefore be rendered: The painter Hubert van Eyck, to whom none is deemed superior, began, and John, who is second to him in art, completed the great

3

work. Judocus Vijt paid for it. He invites you by this verse, on the 6th day of May, to come and contemplate the work.[1] But even that, the key document about Hubert, is not so convincing as it sounds. It was not painted by Jan: a comparison with the many other inscriptions shows that clearly. Some authorities hold that it was rapidly painted by a collaborator for the occasion of the unveiling; others that it is a forgery of a much later date. A copy of the inscription in a manuscript collection of such things made before 1629 gives the first two words of the third line as *frater perfectus*—which is where the brother theory comes in. But this evidence alone is not enough to establish the existence of Hubert. There are, however, several documentary references to a painter called Hubert van Eyck. The usual belief to-day, therefore, is that he did exist, that he was the brother of Jan and that he at least planned *The Holy Lamb*. But which, if any, parts he actually painted is purely a matter of opinion. As we have no authenticated work by him, this opinion must be based on stylistic differences between parts of the altarpiece itself, either in execution or inspiration. Authorities unfortunately do not agree on these differences, and until they do, all attributions of other works to Hubert must be questionable.

We have, on the other hand, nine works definitely signed by Jan (Plates xxvii to xxxvi), and it is on their stylistic character that other works are attributed to him. Those I have chosen for reproduction are the most generally accepted.

The second problem concerns technique. The Italian art historian Giorgio Vasari first stated that the van Eycks used oil, and indeed invented its use. That was in 1568, and his statement has been naively repeated by all but the most careful writers ever since. It is still widely believed, and it is certainly not true. Oil, it seems, was

[1] I accept van Puyvelde's transcription. There are variants.

commonly used in their day, but it is almost certain that they themselves did not use it. But the fact is that we do not know what their exact technique was. Martin Davies, in the new National Gallery catalogue (1945), is content to say of Hubert and Jan that 'no doubt one or the other made some as yet undefinable change in technique' and he describes their works by the non-committal if somewhat unhelpful term 'painted surface'. I have been even more non-committal in the captions, by omitting all reference to medium.

It is a relief to turn from these tiresome problems to the works of art themselves, so serene and solid and assured, so factual. We may find in what we attribute to Hubert a certain poetic quality: indeed, that is the distinction on which many critics base their attributions to him. But he is only poetic in relation to Jan and other Flemings, not to contemporary Italian work. Flemish art is always primarily material: it is concerned with the definition of earthly forms and textures, though not, therefore, necessarily, as we shall see, for a materialist purpose. What the Flemings represent is easily *recognized*: they record the familiar with supreme craftsmanship. That is why they are so popular. 'The vision of these painters was so little removed from the vision we employ for buying stuffs in a shop that it required no effort of reflection to recognize its accuracy and effectiveness' (Roger Fry). And so the tourist in St Bavon, encouraged by the guides, indulges in orgiastic play with a magnifying glass, and pays his simple tribute by saying: 'There's a lot of work in that', as if he were talking about a well-kept ledger.

But the astonishing thing about the great altarpiece is that it is not swamped in this recognizable detail, that the imaginative conception remains clear and noble and profoundly moving in spite of the accumulation of innumerable facts. It is like the work of a major historian. The facts are there, but they are not merely assembled as the minor historian assembles them, as the ledger-clerk assembles his figures; they are kept in their place as things in themselves worthless: they are subordinated to the whole imaginative design; they are the material for the creative artist. As Gibbon, for example, breathed a huge and resplendent life into so many dusty records, so did the van Eycks reveal universal truths through a mass of reported particulars.

The devotees of the magnifying glass are ecstatic over the wrinkles in the face of the Canon van der Paele (Plate xxxii); the mirror or the amber beads by it, or the hairs of the dog in *Giovanni Arnolfini and his Wife* (Plate xxx); the jewels and embroideries of Christ the King (Plate xii); but they fail to see the pictures. But if, it might be argued, the painters did not wish us to examine the detail so closely, why did they lavish such extravagant skill on the rendering of it? I do not say that the detail is not to be examined: I say that it is not *only* the detail that is to be examined. We too must make the synthesis that the painters made: we must see the wood, however many trees they planted in it and however exquisite each tree, each leaf of each tree, each vein of each leaf may be: for they planted those trees to make a wood. That is the difference between the van Eycks and the minor Flemings. These latter were contented, like the foolish tourist, to magnify parts: they had no vision of wholes; they made inventories.

We must remember that the beginning of Flemish painting was in the illuminated manuscript, not, like that of Italian, in the fresco. It lacked—at least, before Rubens—the grandeur of design, the boldness and the noble simplicity which compel even the least sensitive of us to see the whole. We are tempted to turn the pages, as it were; to unfold the picture in time rather than to see all its parts simultaneously. On the other hand, Flemish art has the virtue of discipline: its statements are more positive, more precise, more analytic. It has a solidity and a religious stillness which the more exalted and unstable vision of the Southerner may lack.

It is probably because of the absence of a compelling rhythmic unity that our first impression of *The Holy Lamb* is disappointing. It seems to be but the sum of its parts, a symmetric assemblage of those parts, rather than a composition; for it is that rhythmic unity which should, in a work of art, make the whole greater than the sum of its parts. Indeed, the altarpiece may even be valued below that sum. The proportions of the parts to one another are faulty. The upper panels weigh too heavily on the lower, in particular the upper central panel outweighs the whole; it should not: it should soar above them. A work with such a theme should be essentially up-thrusting: it should have the feel of Salisbury spire; but, to be brutal, it has more that of a pompous department store—a row of massive columns resting apparently on fragile glass. Moreover, it lacks a focus. Our pleasure is taken in passing from panel to panel, turning the pages of the illuminated manuscript, rather than in the contemplation of the whole. But when we have done that, then an *invisible* unity seems to have been conveyed, a pattern in the memory. There has been a slow unfolding which finally achieves *one* most tremendous effect in the imagination. This is largely stimulated by our gradual understanding of the unity of conception. I do not think I can use my remaining space better than in outlining this thematic pattern.

The theme is, of course, the Redemption. When the panels are closed (Plate v), this theme is announced by its Jewish and pagan heralds—the prophets and sibyls, as in Michelangelo's Sistine ceiling.[1] The van Eycks have taken pains to reinforce their meaning by

[1] See *Michelangelo* in this series, Plates xxv–xxxiv.

7

an elaborate series of inscriptions. I have reproduced the most urgent of these in the captions or Notes to the Illustrations. It will be seen, on consulting them, that out of the many possible prophecies, it is those which insist on the *royalty* of Christ that have been chosen. The theme is enriched by this emphasis—that it is a king who shall be the sacrificial Lamb—which was, to the medieval mind, the most tremendous image available of God's condescension.

Below the remoter prophecies we find the immediate Annunciation (Plates vii and viii), the first act of the Redemption itself. Below that again are the two Sts John: the Baptist, as the latest herald, and the Evangelist, as author of *Revelations*, from which the theme of the Lamb is taken (Plate xi). These figures are flanked by Judocus Vijt and his wife, the givers of the altarpiece in thanks for God's gift of Himself (Plates ix and x).

When the wings are opened (Plate vi) the theme is lifted from the historical to the mystic plane. It is not the story of the ministry and suffering of the man Jesus which the van Eycks picture, but its eternal significance. Their language is not narrative, but symbolic. Therefore, central and dominating all by His mass and magnificence, is the enthroned figure of Christ the King (Plate xii), not the broken man on the cross. He has the symbols of spiritual and temporal power, the triple tiara, the sceptre and the crown. He wears the scarlet mantle of authority and is laden with jewels. It is only so, only through these material terms, that the Northern painters can express their vision of divine majesty. While we delight in the exquisite rendering of all this profuse detail, we must still ask whether there is not more majesty in the unadorned Christs of the Italians. Noble, serene, magnificent as this king may be, is He so Godlike as the Christ of Piero della Francesca's *Resurrection*? [1]

[1] Plate xxxiii of *Piero della Francesca* in this series.

8

On Christ's right, the Virgin Mary sits crowned as Queen of Heaven (Plate xiii); on His left, St. John the Baptist, with Isaiah open at Chapter XL: 'Comfort ye, comfort ye, my people . . .' (Plate xiv). Here, then, is the apotheosis in Heaven of those whose mission on earth was expressed on the outer panels. They are flanked by singing and playing angels (Plates xv and xvi), the familiar images of rejoicing. And they, in turn, are flanked by the fallen Adam and Eve, the eternal types of humanity corresponding to the individuals in time, the donor and his wife. Above them are the images of the good and evil in man, the offering of Abel and the sin of Cain: the causes for which God judged man worthy of redemption and in need of it.

It is, then, clear enough that there is a thematic unity between these upper panels, but they remain æsthetically apart. Only the most naive and mechanical symmetry connects them. The lower panels, on the other hand, make a more satisfactory whole, although they are, in their turn, quite unconnected with the upper in design. But in theme, once again, the connection is clear and profound. All here takes place in one wide landscape, the redeemed earth, Paradise regained. In the centre, on the altar, is the Lamb of God, symbol of the passion and the mass, who pours His redeeming blood into the chalice. He is worshipped by angels and flanked by the instruments of His suffering, the cross and the pillar. Before Him is yet another symbol, the Fountain of Life, the source of sanctifying grace. The doctrine of baptism by water is added to that of the holy communion (Plates xix and xx).

The church triumphant approaches this great centre in orderly groups. It has been suggested that these groups at the same time represent the virtues, an interpretation which I add in brackets. To the spectator's right of the fountain are the Apostles with Sts Paul

9

and Barnabas, immediately followed by the Confessors (Plate xxii) (Faith); behind them, in the outer panels, are the Hermits (Temperance) and the Pilgrims (Prudence) (Plate xxvi). On the spectator's left is a similar arrangement. In front are the Prophets and such Gentiles as Virgil, who were held to have foreseen the coming of the Redeemer (Hope) (Plate xxi), and in the outer panels the Knights of Christ and the Just Judges (Justice) (Plate xxv). Finally, emerging from the background are, on the right, the Virgins (Plate xxiv) and on the left the male Martyrs (Plate xxiii) (Charity, interpreted as the love of God).

The van Eycks, then, clearly set out with a didactic purpose. The underlining of their meaning by the inscriptions not only confirms this but proves how important it was to them. It may be difficult for the agnostic to identify himself imaginatively, even by the 'willing suspension of disbelief', with their point of view. In that case he must fail to achieve a comprehensive understanding of this great altarpiece. For him, it falls apart into its component panels, for, as I have said, it lacks formal cohesion. Of each of them, he may say, as of all those other works which I reproduce but have no space to comment on: 'Here are things as they *really* are, not as we normally see them, impressionistically: here are the forms and textures of things defined in the most positive and analytic terms: here is a new realism expressed in draughtsmanship and modelling and colour-gradations: here, in art, is the scientific and enquiring mind invading the world of Gothic vision, which it is to destroy.' He sees the van Eycks as the first great painters who conspicuously pointed the way to materialism. But that is precisely not the way they intended to point. Their attitude was dogmatically, even theologically religious: that is repellent to many people. But to ignore it, as the criticism of thirty years ago tended to do, is as if we ignored the thought of Plato or St Augustine and only praised their style. The significance of an egg is in its eggness: an empty shell is no longer an egg.

References.   The Roger Fry quotation comes from his *Flemish Art*, 1927. The phrase 'the willing suspension of disbelief' is from Coleridge's *Biographia Literaria*, Ch. 14.   The theory is discussed at length by I. A. Richards in *Principles of Literary Criticism*, Ch. XXXII–XXXV, and *Practical Criticism*, Ch. VII.

Notes to the Illustrations

The plates are arranged in four groups: 1. Works plausibly attributed to Hubert and therefore painted before 1426; 2. *The Holy Lamb* and details, a joint work; 3. Works signed and dated by Jan; 4. Works generally attributed to Jan.

The medium employed is not specified. See Introduction, page 4

Plates V–XXVI.

The history of this altarpiece may be summarized as follows:

1432. Completed.

1566. Hidden from iconoclasts.

1584. Set up again in Ghent.

1781. The Emperor Joseph II shocked by Adam and Eve had these panels stored away.

1794. Four centre panels taken to Paris by Commissioners of French Republic. Wings stored with church archives.

1816. Centre panels returned to Ghent and exhibited in Museum. In the meantime the vicar-general of St Bavon had sold the wings, less Adam and Eve. They passed through the hands of a Brussels merchant and an English collector to the King of Prussia, from whom they went to the Berlin Museum.

1861. Adam and Eve acquired by the Musée des Beaux Arts, Brussels.

1919. Berlin wings ceded to Belgian government under Treaty of Versailles (Article 247). Whole work reassembled at St Bavon.

1934. Panel of *Just Judges* stolen and never recovered.

1940. Whole altarpiece removed for safety to Pau, France, where it was later seized by Hitler and hidden in salt-mines at Alt-Ausee, Tyrol.

1945. Recovered by Belgian forces and reassembled in St Bavon.

There is evidence that the altarpiece had a predella, representing Hell or Limbo. The latter seems more probable, its theme being Redemption.

The inscriptions, in these notes and in captions, are given as painted, the omitted letters in brackets. I have only had space to translate where a Biblical reference cannot be given.

Plate V.

The scrolls in the Sibyl panels (top centre) read: NIL MORTALE SONA(N)S AFFLATA ES NUMINE (Pronouncing no human words, thou art inspired by Divinity: Virgil, Aeneid, vi. 50, slightly altered), and REX ADVE(N)IET (PER) SEC(V)LA FVTVR(VS) SCI(LI)C(ET) I(N) CARN(E) (Thy king shall come who shall endure down the ages, namely in the flesh: *Oracula Sibyllina*, quoted by St Augustine in *De Civitate Dei*, verse 2).

Plate XII.

On stole: SABOTÂ (Lord of Hosts).

On lower border of mantle: ANANXIN + PEX + PE(R)V(M) + Δ . . . + PE . . . NC + ANANX . . . (Power, King of kings, Lord, King of kings, Power).

On steps of throne: VITA SINE MORTE IN CAPITE IVVE(N)T(VS) S(I)N(E) SENECTVTE I(N) FRONTE GAVDIV(M) S(I)N(E) MERORE A DEXTRIS SECVRITAS S(I)N(E) TI(M)ORE A SINIST(RI)S (On His head life without death, on His brow youth without age, on His right joy without sorrow, on His left security without fear).

Plate XIV.

On open book: CONSOLAMI(NI), opening of Isaiah xl. 1, followed by an impression of Gothic writing.

Plates XIX and XX.

On antependium of altar, across: ECCE AGNUS DEI QUI TOLLIT PEC(CA)TA MV(N)DI (John i. 29). Left pendant: IHES(VS) VIA and right pendant: VITA, V(ER)ITA(S) (John xiv. 6).

On margin of fountain: HIC EST FONS ATQUE VIT(A)E PROCEDENS DE SEDE DEI: (AGNI). The last word is inexplicably altered to HONI (Ref. Rev. xxii. 1).

The buildings of the heavenly Jerusalem in the background cannot be identified with any certainty. There are elements from Cologne and Utrecht.

Plate XXV.

On frame: CHRISTI MILITES and JUSTI JUDICI (Knights of Christ and Just Judges). On shield of centre knight: D(OMINV)S FORTIS ADONAY SABAOT V . . . EM(MANV)EL I.H.S. XRI AGLA (God Almighty, Lord of Hosts, Emanuel,

Jesus Christ, Agla). Agla is a word composed of the first letters of the Hebrew *atah gebir leilam adonai* (Thou art eternally powerful, Lord). It was frequently used in the Middle Ages as a name for God.

Plate XXVI.

On frame: HEREMITE S(AN)CTI and PE(RE)GRINI S(AN)C(T)I (Holy Hermits and Holy Pilgrims).

Very divergent attempts have been made to identify the personages in the last two plates. Among others, the foreground figure in *Just Judges* has been identified as Hubert van Eyck, and the man looking back with a rosary round his neck as Jan. But the latter has also been recognized as Henry V of England!

Plate XXVII.

On parapet: TYM, ωΘEOC and LEAL SOVVENIR, which is obscure. It may suggest that the sitter was called Timothy, but why partly in a sort of Greek lettering?

Plate XXVIII.

Inscribed with Jan's motto, *Als ikh kan*, which is believed to refer to a Flemish proverb: As I can, but not as I would. Jan wrote this in a curious semi-Greek lettering: AΛC. IXH. XAN.

Plate XXIX.

Inscribed as Plate XXVIII.

Plate XXX

Arnolfini was an Italian merchant who lived in Bruges from 1421 to 1470. There are various theories about the precise significance of this work, for which the reader is referred to the National Gallery catalogue *Early Netherlandish School*, 1945.

Plate XXXIII.

de Leeuw (1401–after 1459) was a gold- and silversmith of Bruges. The frame is inscribed with a rhyming quatrain in Flemish giving the date of his birth and the painter's name.

Plate XXXV.

Inscribed as Plate XXVIII

Plate XXXVI.

Belonged formerly to the Bruges Guild of Painters and Saddlers, who exposed it in their chapel on St Luke's day. It was lost, but discovered in the fish market in 1808. A Latin inscription indicates that Margaret was thirty-three at the time, and is followed by the motto as in Plate XXVIII.

Plate XXXVII.

Left wing of a triptych. Inscribed: AVE GRA(TIA) PLENA and ECCE ANCILLA D(OMI)NI, inverted. Compare Plates VII and VIII.

Plates XXXIX and XL.

Frames inscribed with passages from Wisdom vii. 29 and 26 (compare Plate XIII) and Ecclesiasticus xxiv. 23, 24, etc., too long for quotation here. They will be found in Weale. Scroll in Plate XL inscribed: DISCITE A ME QUIA MITIS SUM ET HUMILIS CORDE (Matthew xi. 29).

Plate XLII.

Formerly in Collegiate Church of Our Lady, Autun. Along lower border of Virgin's mantle is a text from the Lesson at Matins in the office of Our Lady. The town seems to be based on Maastricht. Rolin (1376–1462) was a Chancellor of Burgundy and Brabant from 1422. He founded the famous hospital at Beaune.

Plate XLVII.

The sitter wears the collar of the Order of St Anthony, founded in 1382 by Albert of Bavaria.

Plate XLVIII.

De Lannoy (1386/7–1474) carries wand of office as Chamberlain to Duke of Burgundy, and wears order of the Golden Fleece; therefore painted after 1431, when he received that collar from a Bruges goldsmith. He was Lord of Malembaix and Governor of Lille.

I. THE THREE MARIES AT THE SEPULCHRE. By Hubert van Eyck. Oak. 71 × 89 cm. Vierhouten, Holland. Coll. D. G. Beuningen. Formerly Sir Francis Cook, Richmond.

II. (*Opposite*) THE CRUCIFIXION AND LAST JUDGMENT. By Hubert van Eyck. Canvas transferred from panel. 62 × 25 cm. New York, Metropolitan Museum

III. THE CRUCIFIXION. By Hubert van Eyck. Linen, transferred from panel. 43 × 26 cm. Berlin. Gemäldegalerie.

IV. THE VIRGIN AND CHILD IN A CHURCH.
By Hubert or Jan van Eyck. Oak. 31 × 14 cm.
Berlin, Gemäldegalerie.

V. (*Opposite*) THE HOLY LAMB. Wings closed. By Hubert and Jan van Eyck. Completed 1432. Oak. Ghent, Church of St Bavon. See Plates VI–XI and *Notes*.

VI. THE HOLY LAMB. Wings open. By Hubert and Jan van Eyck. Completed 1432. Oak. Ghent, Church of St Bavon. See Plates XII–XXVI.

VII. THE ANGEL OF THE
ANNUNCIATION WITH
ZACHARIAS ABOVE. From
Plate V. Angel, 47×27 cm.
Zacharias, 13×27 cm. (Photo:
W. F. Mansell.)

On scroll: EXULTA SATIS FILIA
SYO(N) IVBILA ECCE REX TUUS
VE(N)IT (Zach. ix. 9).

Behind angel, continuing to
adjoining panel: AVE GRACIA
PLENA D(OMI)N(V)S TECV(M)
(Luke i. 28).

VIII. THE VIRGIN OF THE
ANNUNCIATION WITH
MICAH ABOVE. From Plate
V. Virgin, 47×27 cm. Micah,
13×27 cm. (Photo: W. F.
Mansell.)
On scroll: EX TE EGREDIETUR
QUI SIT DOMINATOR IN ISR(AEL)S
(Micah v. 2).
Behind Virgin, inverted: ECCE
ANCILLA D(OMI)NI (Luke i. 38).

IX. (*Opposite*) JUDOCUS VIJT AND HIS WIFE, ISABELLE BORLUUT, DONORS OF THE HOLY LAMB. From Plate V. Each 57×20 cm. (Photos: W. F. Mansell.)

X. HEAD OF JUDOCUS VIJT. Detail from opposite plate.
The name is variously spelt. Vijt was of a prosperous merchant family. He was burgomaster of Ghent in 1433 and died *c.* 1439.

XI. ST JOHN THE BAPTIST AND ST JOHN THE EVANGELIST. From
Plate V. Each 57×20 cm. (Photos: W. F. Mansell.)

XII CHRIST THE KING. From Plate VI 82 × 31 cm. The cloth of honour is decorated with a repeated device composed of the symbolic pelican, vine-leaves and grapes and a scroll inscribed: IHESVS XPS (Jesus Christ). This weighs heavily against the old description of the figure as that of God the Father. See also Plate XVIII and *Notes* for the inscriptions. (Photo: *Picture Post* Library.)

XIII. THE VIRGIN MARY.
From Plate VI. 65×28 cm.
(Photo: *Picture Post* Library.)
On arches: HEC E(ST)
SPECIOSIOR SOLE + SUP(ER)
O(MN)EM STELLARV(M)
DISPOSIC(I)O(N)E(M) LUCI
(C)O(M)PA(RA)TA I(N)VE(N)IT-
(VR) P(RI)OR CA(N)DOR E(ST)
E(N)IM LVCIS ETERN(A)E +
SPEC(VL)VM S(I)N(E) MAC(V)LA
DEI (MAIESTATIS) (Wisdom vii.
29 and 26).
On the cloth of honour is
indecipherable writing in
Saracenic characters.

XIV. ST JOHN THE BAPTIST.
From Plate VI. 65 × 28 cm.
(Photo: *Picture Post* Library.)
On arches: HIC E(ST) BAPTISTA
IOH(ANN)ES: MAIOR HO(M)-
I(N)E: PAR ANG(E)LIS: LEGIS
SV(M)MA: EWA(N)GELII
SA(NC)TIO AP(OSTO)LOR(VM)
VOX: SILE(N)CIV(M) P(RO)
PHETAR(VM): LUCERNA MVN(DI)
D(O)M(I)NI TESTIS (This is John
the Baptist, greater than man,
equal to the angels, the sum of
the law, the sanction of the
gospels, the voice of the Apos-
tles, the silence of the prophets,
the lamp of the world, the
witness of the Lord (Sermon
of Petrus Chrysologus, Arch-
bishop of Ravenna, on Behead-
ing of St John the Baptist.
Migne, *Patres Latini*, T.52).
See *Notes*.

XV. SINGING ANGELS.
From Plate VI. 63 × 27
cm.
On frame: MELOS DEO
LAUS P(ER)HEN(N)IS
GRA(TIA)R(VM) A(CT)IO
(Melody, praise to God,
eternal thanksgiving).
Source unknown.

XVI. MUSICIAN ANGELS.
From Plate VI. 63×27 cm.
(Photo: W. F. Mansell.)
On frame: LAUDAT(E) EV(M)
IN CORDIS ET ORGANO (Psalm
cl. 4).

XVII. ADAM WITH ABEL'S OFFERING ABOVE, and EVE WITH THE MURDER OF ABEL ABOVE. From Plate VI. Each 80 × 13 cm. (Photos: W. F. Mansell.)

On frame below Adam: ADAM NOS I(N) MORTE(M) P(RE)CIPITA(VI)T (Adam hurled us unto death). Source unknown.

On frame below Eve: EVA OCCIDENDO OBFUIT (Eve by succumbing betrayed us: St Augustine in *The Annunciation of the Incarnation*).

XVIII. HEAD OF CHRIST THE KING. Detail of Plate XII.
The Inscription reads : + HIC E(ST) DEUS POTE(N)TISSIM(US) PP (PROPTER) DIVINA(M)
MAIESTATE(M) + SV(MMVS) O(MN)I(V)M OPTI(MVS) PP (PROPTER) DVLCEDI(NI)S
BO(N)ITATE(M) + REMVNERATOR LIBERALISSIMVS PROPTER IM(M)ENSAM LARGITATEM
(This is God, all powerful in His divine majesty, the first of all, the best in the
goodness of His loving-kindness, the most liberal rewarder in His infinite bounty).

XIX. THE HOLY LAMB. From Plate VI. 53 × 93 cm. (Photo: W. F. Mansell.) For inscriptions, see *Notes*.

XX. THE HOLY LAMB. Detail of opposite plate. (Photo: W. F. Mansell.)

XXI. THE PROPHETS AND PRECURSORS. Detail of Plate XIX. (Photo: W. F. Mansell.)

XXII. THE APOSTLES AND CONFESSORS. Detail of Plate XIX. (Photo: W. F. Mansell.)

XXIII. THE MARTYRS. Detail of Plate XIX. (Photo: W. F. Mansell.)

XXIV. THE HOLY VIRGINS. Detail of Plate XIX. (Photo: W. F. Mansell.)

XXV. THE JUST JUDGES AND THE KNIGHTS OF CHRIST. From Plate VI. Each
57×20 cm. (Photo: *Picture Post* Library.) See *Notes*.

XXVI. THE HERMITS AND THE PILGRIMS. From Plate VI. Each 57×20 cm. (Photo: *Picture Post* Library.) See *Notes*.

XXVII. PORTRAIT OF A YOUNG MAN. By Jan van Eyck.
Signed and dated 1432. Oak. 34 × 19 cm. London, National
Gallery.

XXVIII. THE VIRGIN AND CHILD (known as *The Ince Hall Madonna*). By Jan van Eyck. Signed and dated 1433. 22×15 cm. Melbourne, National Gallery. (Photo: *Picture Post* Library.) See *Notes*.

XXIX. A MAN IN A TURBAN. By Jan van Eyck. Signed and dated 1433.
Oak. 25×19 cm. London, National Gallery.

XXX. GIOVANNI ARNOLFINI AND HIS WIFE, GIOVANNA CENAMI.
By Jan van Eyck. Signed and dated 1434. Oak. 81 × 59 cm. London, National
Gallery. Compare Plate XLVI and see *Notes*.

XXXI. (*Opposite*) THE VIRGIN AND CHILD, WITH STS DONATIAN AND GEORGE, AND THE DONOR, CANON G. VAN DER PAELE. By Jan van Eyck. Signed and dated 1436. Oak. 122 × 157 cm. Bruges Museum.

XXXII. CANON VAN DER PAELE. Detail from opposite plate.

XXXIII. THE GOLDSMITH JAN DE LEEUW. By Jan van Eyck. Signed and
dated 1436. Oak. 33×27 cm. Vienna, Kunsthistorisches Museum. (Photo:
Picture Post Library.) See *Notes*.

XXXIV. ST BARBARA.
By Jan van Eyck. Signed
and dated 1437. Oak.
32 × 18 cm. Antwerp
Museum. (Photo:
Picture Post Library.)

XXXV. THE VIRGIN OF THE FOUNTAIN. By Jan van Eyck.
Signed and dated 1439. Oak. 19 × 12 cm. Antwerp Museum. (Photo:
Picture Post Library.)

XXXVI. MARGARET VAN EYCK, WIFE OF THE ARTIST. By Jan van Eyck.
Signed and dated 1439. Oak. 32×26 cm. Bruges Museum. (Photo: W. F.
Mansell.) See *Notes*.

XXXVII. THE ANNUNCIA-
TION. By Jan van Eyck.
Canvas transferred from panel.
93 × 36 cm. Washington,
National Gallery of Art,
Mellon Coll. See *Notes*.

XXXVIII. (*Opposite*) THE
ANNUNCIATION. Wings of
Plate XL, closed. By Jan van
Eyck. Oak. Each 27×8 cm.
Dresden, Gemäldegalerie.
(Photo: W. F. Mansell.)

XXXIX. STS MICHAEL AND CATHERINE. Wings of opposite plate, open. Oak.
Each 27×8 cm. Dresden, Gemäldegalerie. (Photo: *Picture Post* Library.)

XL. THE VIRGIN ENTHRONED. Centre of Triptych of which Plates XXXVIII and XXXIX are the wings, closed and open. By Jan van Eyck. Oak. 27×21 cm. Dresden, Gemäldegalerie. (Photo: *Picture Post* Library.) See *Notes*.

XLI. (*Opposite*) VIRGIN AND CHILD (Known as the *Lucca Madonna* because formerly owned by Charles Louis, Duke of Lucca). By Jan van Eyck. Oak. 65×49 cm. Frankfort-on-Main, Städelsches Kunstinstitut. (Photo: *Picture Post* Library.)

XLII. THE VIRGIN AND CHILD WITH THE CHANCELLOR ROLIN. By Jan van Eyck. Oak. 66×62 cm. Paris, Louvre. (Photo: W. F. Mansell.) See *Notes*.

XLIII. ST FRANCIS RECEIVING THE STIGMATA. By Jan van Eyck. Oak. 12×14 cm.
Philadelphia, John G. Johnson Coll.

XLIV. (*Opposite*) NICHOLAS ALBERGATI, CARDINAL OF SANTA CROCE. By Jan van
Eyck. Probably 1432. Oak. 34×27 cm. Vienna, Kunsthistorisches Museum.
Albergati was born in 1375, became Procurator-General of Carthusian order in 1407,
Bishop of Bologna in 1417 and Cardinal in 1462. He was Ambassador to the King of
England in 1431. Van Eyck probably painted him at Bruges in that year. There is a silver
point drawing for this portrait at Dresden.

XLV. PORTRAIT OF A GOLDSMITH. By Jan van Eyck. Oak. 17×11 cm. Sitiu,
Bruckenthal Museum. Formerly Hermannstadt, Gymnasium (Photo: W. F.
Mansell.)
Dürer's cypher and the date 1497 added by an unknown hand.

XLVI. GIOVANNI ARNOLFINI. By Jan van Eyck. Oak. 29×20 cm. Berlin, Gemäldegalerie. Compare Plate XXX.

XLVII. THE MAN WITH THE PINK. By Jan van Eyck. Oak 40×31 cm. Berlin, Gemäldegalerie. See *Notes*.

XLVIII. SIR BALDWIN DE LANNOY By Jan van Eyck Oak. 26 × 20 cm.
Berlin, Gemäldegalerie. See *Notes*.

Biographical Notes

Nothing substantial is known of Hubert and attempts have even been made to prove that he never existed, e.g. by E. Renders, 1933. He is believed to have died in 1426

JAN VAN EYCK

Date and place of birth unknown. Latter was perhaps Maaseyck, near Maastricht.

1422–44. Worked at the Hague for John the Merciless, of Bavaria, Count of Holland.

1425. 19 May. At Bruges. Appointed valet de chambre and court painter to Philip the Good, Duke of Burgundy.

1425–30. Visited Lille, Tournay, Lisbon and other places on secret missions for the Duke.

1432. Bought a house at Bruges.

1434. First child born, to whom the Duke stood godfather.

1441. 9 July. Died. Duke granted pension to widow and children.

Bibliographical Notes

Writing on the van Eycks is so voluminous that I think it best to confine myself to mentioning the major English authority:

Weale, W. H. James. *Hubert and Jan van Eyck. Their Life and Work.* 1908. An authoritative and massive work, fully illustrated and with commented bibliography of nearly sixty pages.

Weale, W. H. J., and Brockwell. *The van Eycks and Their Art.* Revised edition of above. 1912.

A recent work by Charles de Tolnay (1939) gives an up-to-date bibliography. Many useful references will also be found in the National Gallery catalogue *Early Netherlandish School*, 1945, including a brief bibliography of the most important works on the Netherlands school (page 118). The following is a well-illustrated and scholarly 'popular' survey:

van Puyvelde, Leo. *The Flemish Primitives.* English ed., 1948.